Ecosystem Facts That You S

The Desert and Grasslands Edition

Nature Picture Books
Children's Nature Books

BABY PROFESSOR
EDUCATION KIDS

Speedy Publishing LLC
40 E. Main St. #1156
Newark, DE 19711
www.speedypublishing.com

The Earth has wide-open spaces, but they can be very different in temperature, what grows there, and who lives there. Come on a trip to the deserts and grasslands of our planet!

Sahara Desert

What makes a Desert?

Not all deserts are like sandy beaches with no ocean. Lots of deserts are miles and miles of rocks and small stones, with a few plants here and there. There are even some deserts in cold regions of the planet.

Peru Desert

What makes a desert, wherever it is on the Earth, is the lack of rain. Deserts usually get less than 10 inches of rainfall each year. Most deserts have very little ground water, and few rivers running through them. Even deserts on the edge of the ocean, like the Namib Desert in Africa, do not gain very much moisture from the sea.

Desert soil is hard and dry, or grainy and dry if it is a desert with sand dunes. The heat can be so high during the day that even if it should rain, often the rain evaporates back up into the air before it even hits the ground.

There are deserts on every continent except Europe, including the Mohave Desert in North America, the Altacama Desert high in South America's mountains, the Gobi Desert stretching across central Asia, and the ten deserts of Australia.

Both Hot and Cold

Although deserts can be desperately hot during the day, they can be dangerously cold at night. The low humidity means that the ground and the air let go of their heat as soon as the sun sets.

Sahara Desert

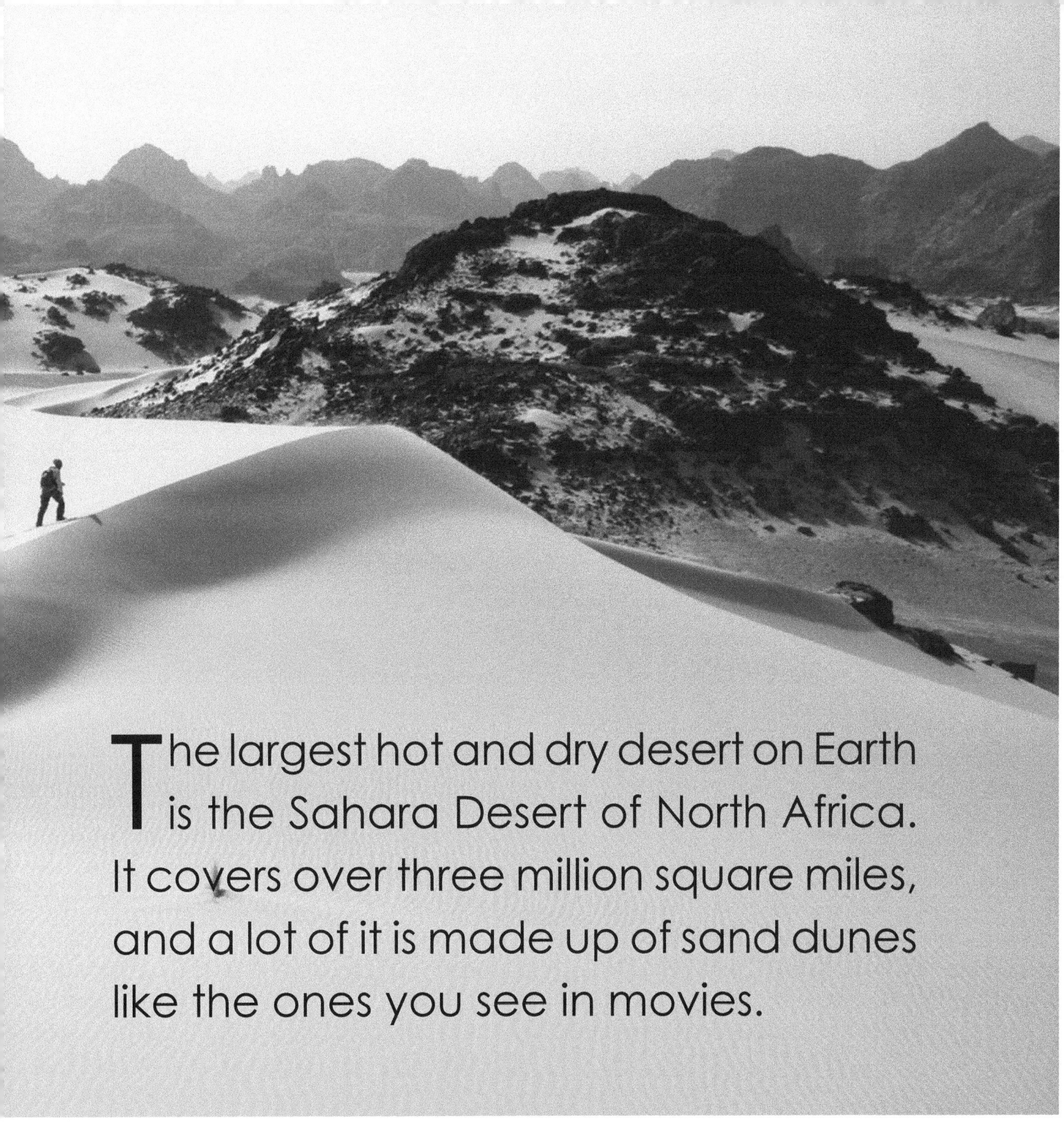

The largest hot and dry desert on Earth is the Sahara Desert of North Africa. It covers over three million square miles, and a lot of it is made up of sand dunes like the ones you see in movies.

Dust storm in Black Rocks Desert

Dust Storms

When a big wind builds up, it can pick up dust, sand, and even small stones off the dry desert surface. Huge dust storms can develop and can grow a mile into the air. Some dust storms travel thousands of miles before they blow out, dropping desert sand and debris far from where the storm had picked it up. Dust from the Sahara Desert sometimes lands on Beijing, the capital of China!

Life in the Desert

But even in the driest, hottest, meanest desert, there is life! Animals, insects, and plants have evolved to take advantage of this hostile environment.

Desert Iguana

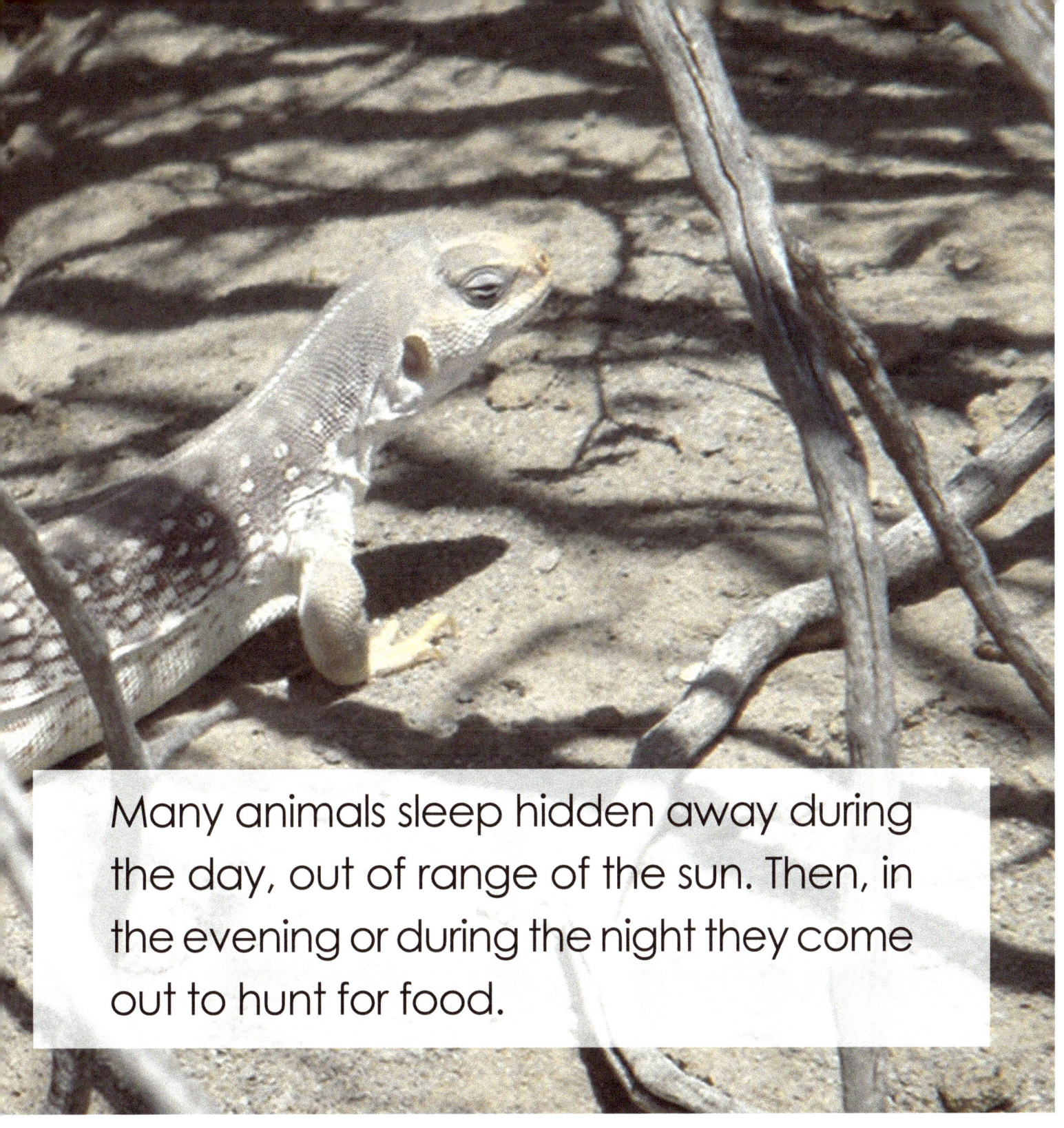

Many animals sleep hidden away during the day, out of range of the sun. Then, in the evening or during the night they come out to hunt for food.

Desert animals have evolved to live on less water than their cousins do in forests or grasslands. Some get all the moisture their body needs from the food they eat. Others, like the camel, store up water when they can find it, so they have it during dry times.

Plants adapt to desert life the same way animals do. Cactus plants store up water in their hollow barrels. Some other plants stay dormant, even for years at a time, until there is some rain. Then they grow and put out flowers very quickly to make use of the energy boost the water has given them.

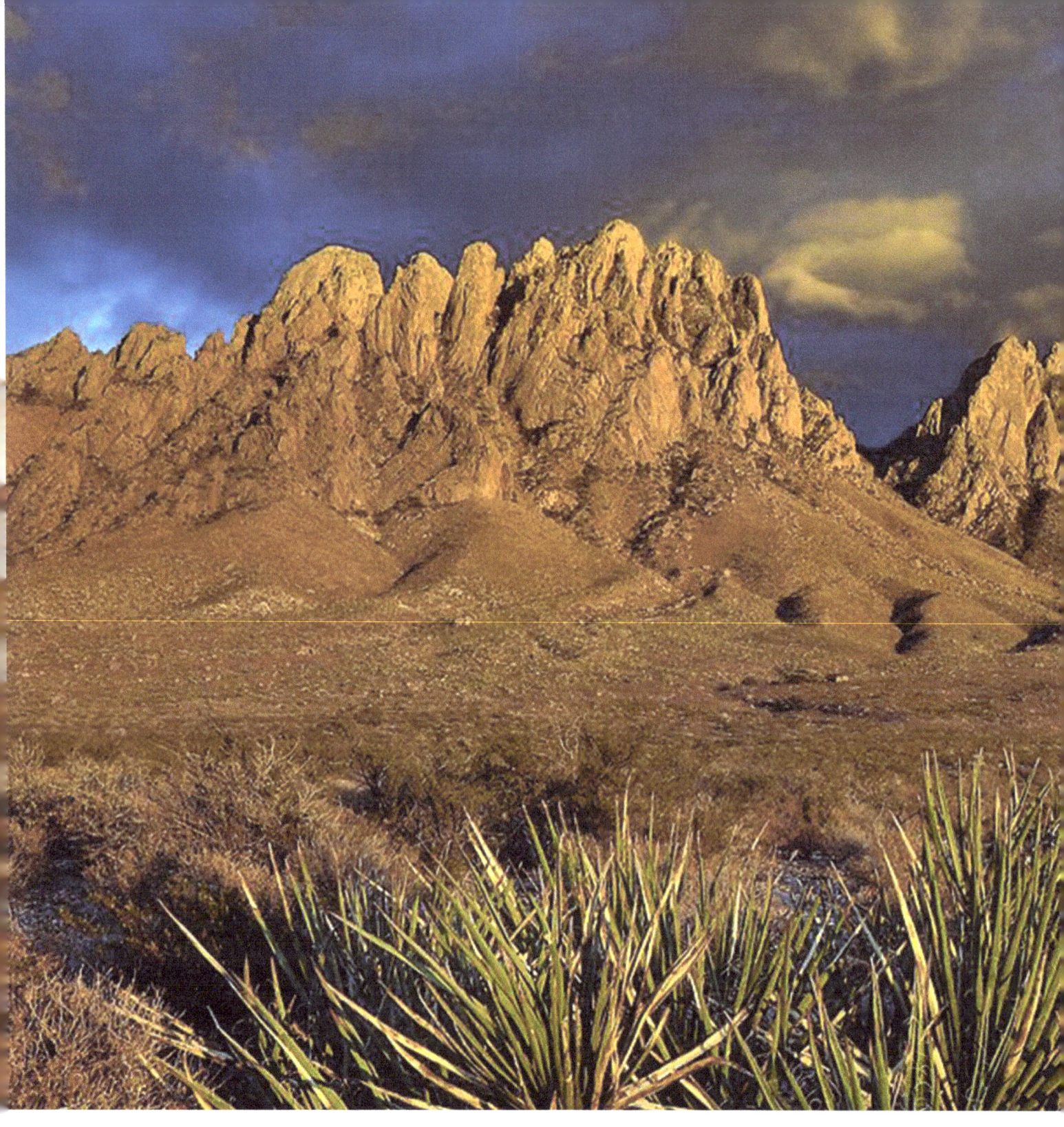

Desert plants also have a wide root system to collect moisture from the ground over a wide area--this is why each plant tends to be quite a distance from the next ones.

Desert Yucca Brevifolia

Desert Animal and Plant Facts

Here are some neat facts about the animals and plants that live in the desert.

Tall Cactus

The giant saguaro cactus can reach 50 feet high, and can live for more than 200 years.

Deep Roots

Growing in the other direction, some desert trees have roots that search 30 feet deep or more to find the water the tree needs.

Secure

The elf owl often makes its home inside a cactus plant, where the thorns will keep it safe from most attackers. Then it flies out at night to find food.

Thirsty

When a camel has the chance, it can swallow as much as 30 gallons of water in fifteen minutes.

Desert Ostriches

Fast Runners

Ostriches can run up to 40 miles an hour, which puts them among the fastest animals in the Sahara Desert. They have excellent hearing and vision, so they can see predators from a long way away and then run in the other direction. If they do get attacked, they can fight back by kicking.

Deserts are Growing

Over 20% of the Earth's dry land is desert, and the deserts are growing. Climate change is disrupting weather patterns, causing some areas to get even less rain than the small amount that had been expecting. The Sahara Desert is getting about 30 miles larger every year. Countries in Africa are trying to plant a huge belt of trees all along the southern edge of the Sahara to slow down its advance.

Where are the Grasslands?

There are two types of grasslands: temperate and tropical. To learn about the tropical grasslands, also called savannas, read the Baby Professor book *Ecosystem Facts That You Should Know - The Savanna and Tundra Edition.*

Taita Hills

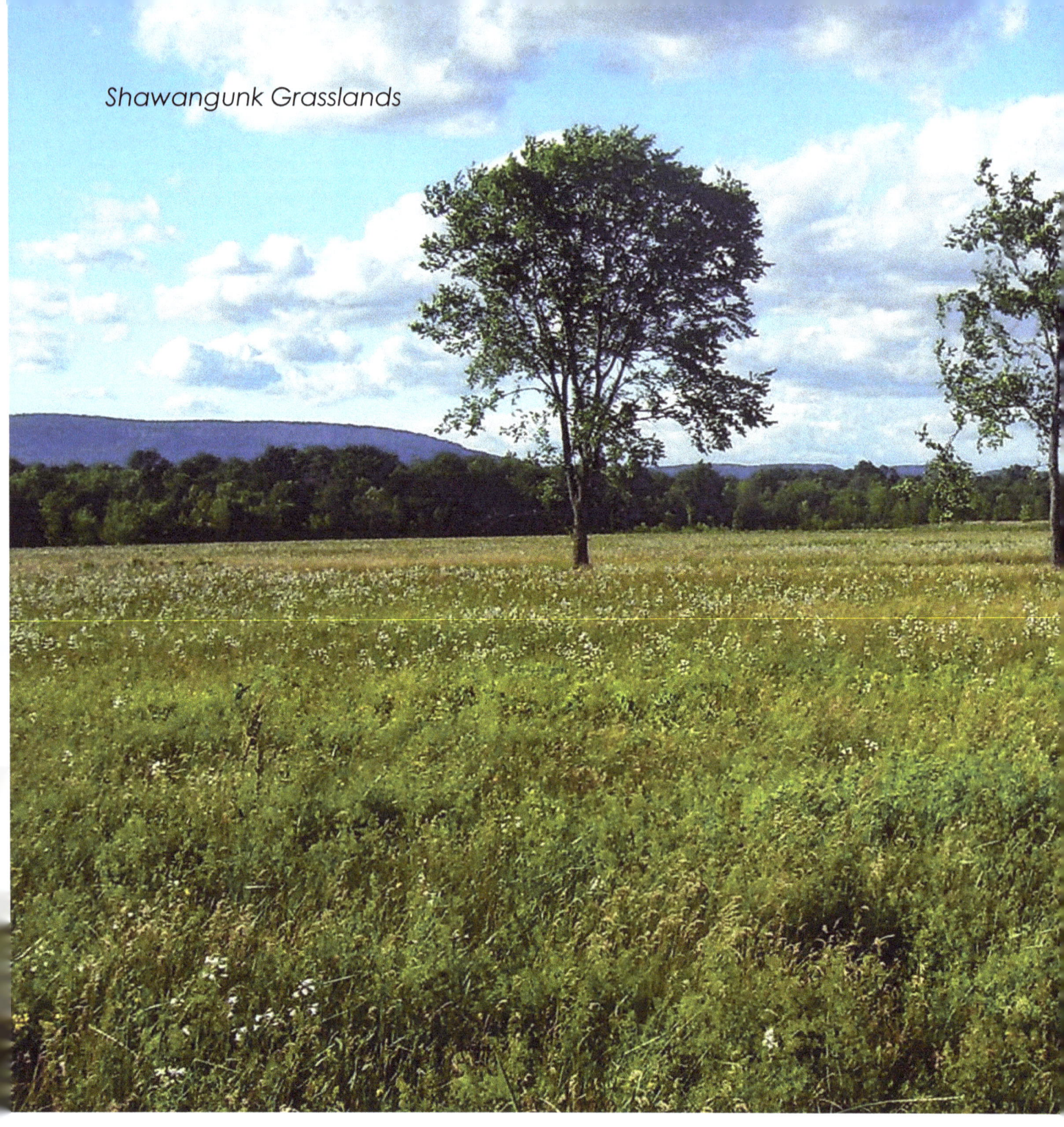

Shawangunk Grasslands

Temperate Grasslands

Temperate grasslands are wide areas of plants like grasses and wildflowers, with not many trees. There is not enough rainfall to support a forest of trees, but there is enough rain to keep the area from becoming a desert.

Grasslands usually lie between deserts and forests. There are broad grasslands in North America, in Uruguay and Argentina in South America, and across southern Russia and Mongolia. Every continent except Antarctica has one of the two types of grasslands.

Living in the Grasslands

Grasslands tend to have hot summers and cold winters. There is little to slow down the wind, so some areas even have tornado or hurricane seasons each year.

A major grassland danger is fire. Once a fire catches among the grasses and shrubs, it can quickly grow up into a major blaze that burns hundreds of acres and sends animals fleeing for shelter. The fires can spread at over 600 feet a minute!

However, grassland plants have adapted to recover quickly from such events, which even make the soil richer, and within a couple of years after a prairie fire the grassland is thick with plants and animals again.

San Raphael Grasslands

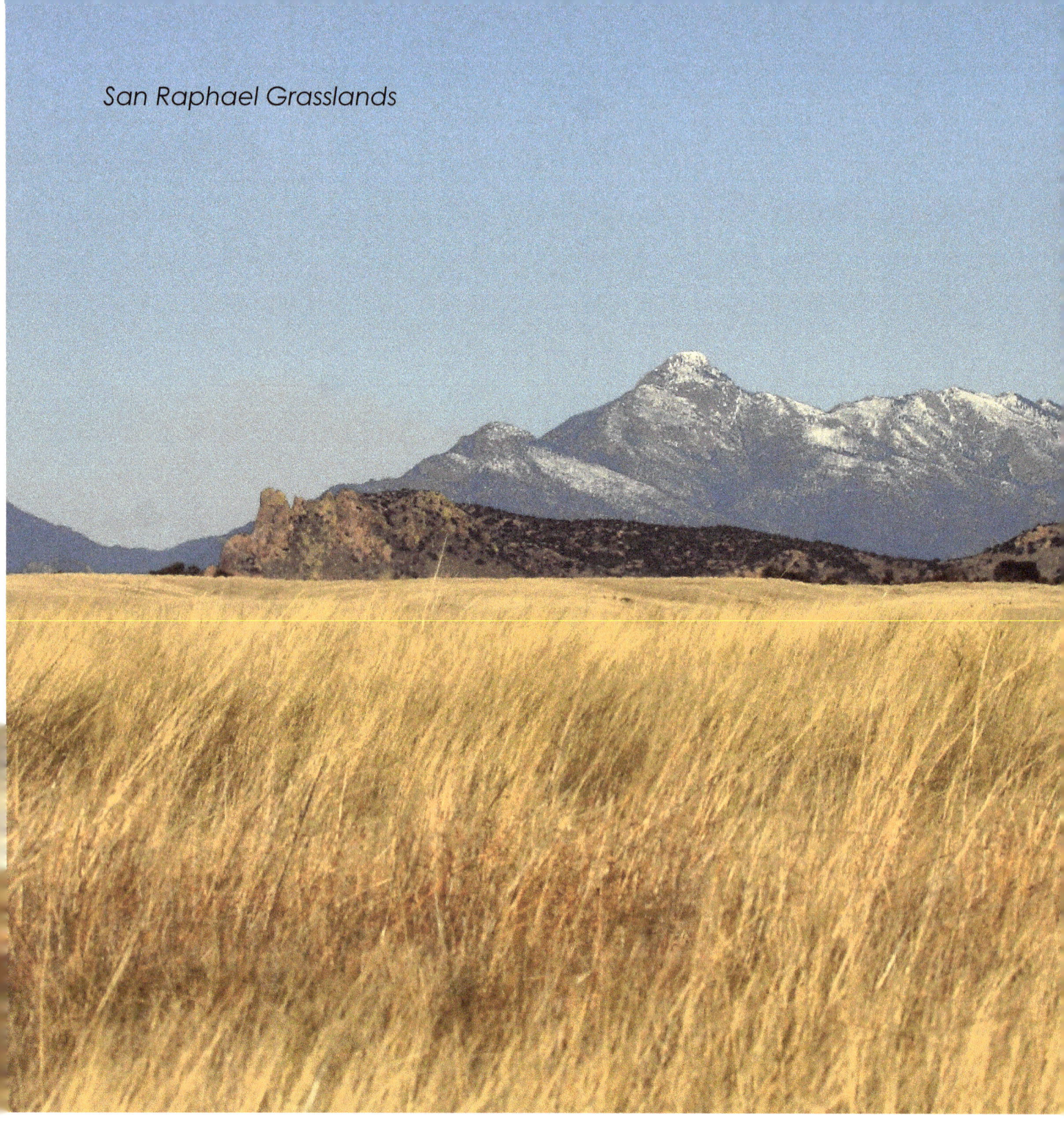

People use the grasslands to grow crops like wheat and corn, and to raise livestock like cattle. The pressure to grow more food is putting the wild grasslands in danger. Moreover, if the grassland is over-grazed it has trouble recovering. In many ways, herds of animals like cows and sheep are more dangerous to the grassland than forest fires are!

Grassland Animals and Plants

Here is an introduction to grassland plants and animals. Grasslands tend to have large herds or communities of a relatively small number of types of animals. For example, in North America, there were only two main grazing animals, buffalo and pronghorn sheep, before people imported sheep and cattle.

Deers in Grassland

Prairie dogs and gophers provide food for carnivores like wolves, coyotes, badgers, and ferrets. Birds include hawks, owls, quails, and sparrows.

Many Kinds of Grass

There are thousands of types of grasses that cover the grasslands. Depending on the amount of water and the shape of the land, the grasses can grow six feet tall.

Where there is not much water the grasses grow no more than two feet tall.

Grasses in the prairies have many romantic names, like needle grass, switchgrass, blue grama grass, and buffalo grass.

Theodore Roosevelt National Park

Grasses tend to have two seasons: when they are growing and when they are dormant. They don't have leaves to shed like trees, and most do not have significant displays of flowers.

Forbs

Forbs are plants like sunflowers. They have soft stems and lots of leaves, and often grow to be the tallest thing in their part of the grassland.

Prairie Towns

Prairie dogs can develop communities of burrows that hold thousands of animals and extend over hundreds of acres. Scientists estimate that at one point the prairies of what is now the United States would have been home to a billion prairie dogs.

Other animals, like foxes and owls, rely on prairie dogs for their food

Fox in Grassland

Large Herds

Bison herds numbering in the millions once lived in the prairies of North America. They were mostly killed in the 1800s, once Europeans settled in the continent and brought guns to hunt with.

Grasslands are Shrinking

People are using more and more of the temperate grasslands for farming, ranching, and for building cities. They are easier to use than mountainsides or desert areas!

But the grasslands are an important part of the whole system of our Earth. If they disappear, it is not just the grasses that will suffer.

Learn more about the Earth, our home!

What part of the world do you live in? Is it forest or grassland, desert or tundra, or something else? Read more Baby Professor books, like *Ecosystem Facts That You Should Know - The Forests Edition* and *Ecosystem Facts That You Should Know - The Savanna and Tundra Edition*, to learn about other parts of the world.

Lightning Source UK Ltd.
Milton Keynes UK
UKHW051853260420
362148UK00009B/45

9 781541 940253